We hope you enjoy coloring this book.

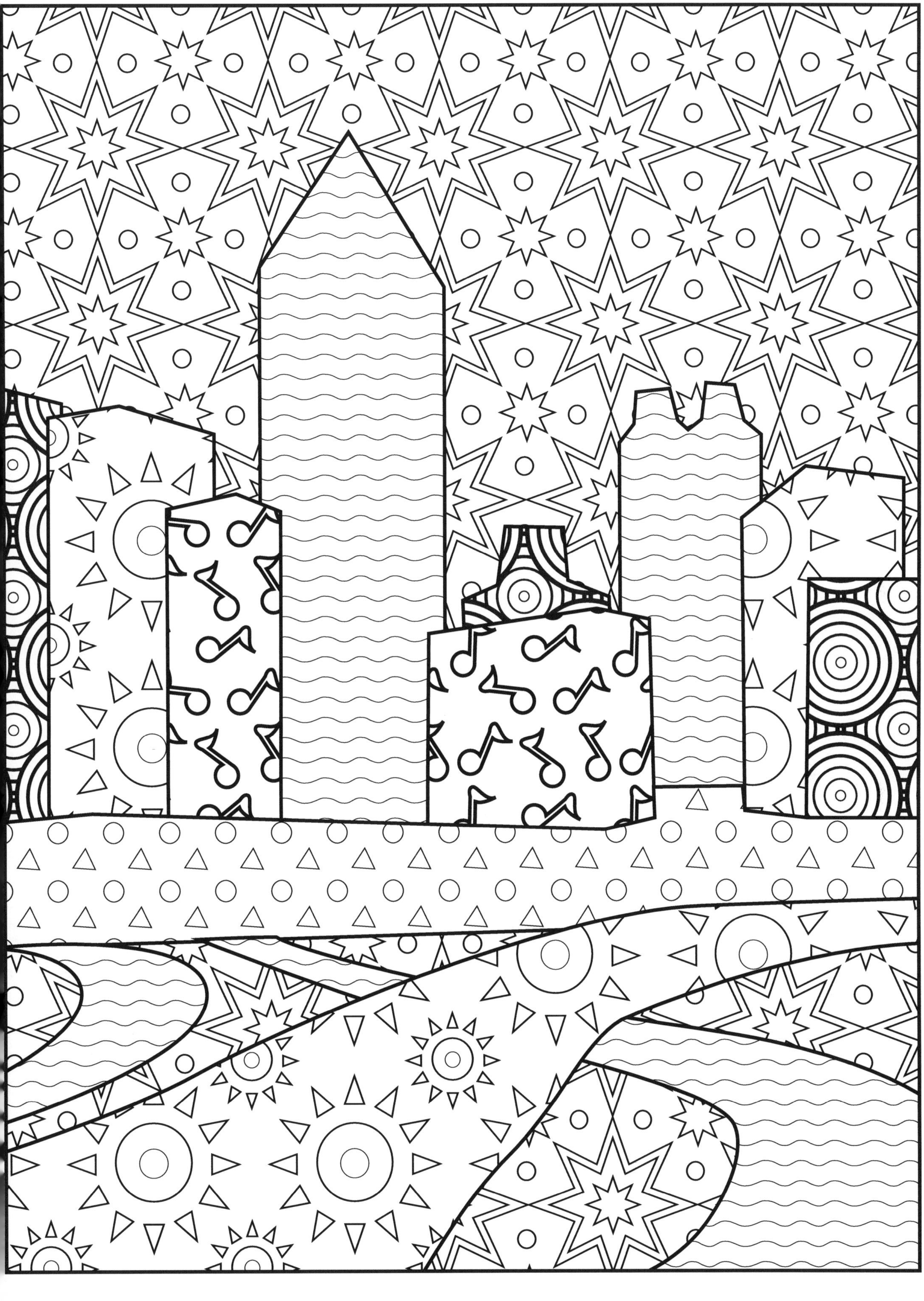

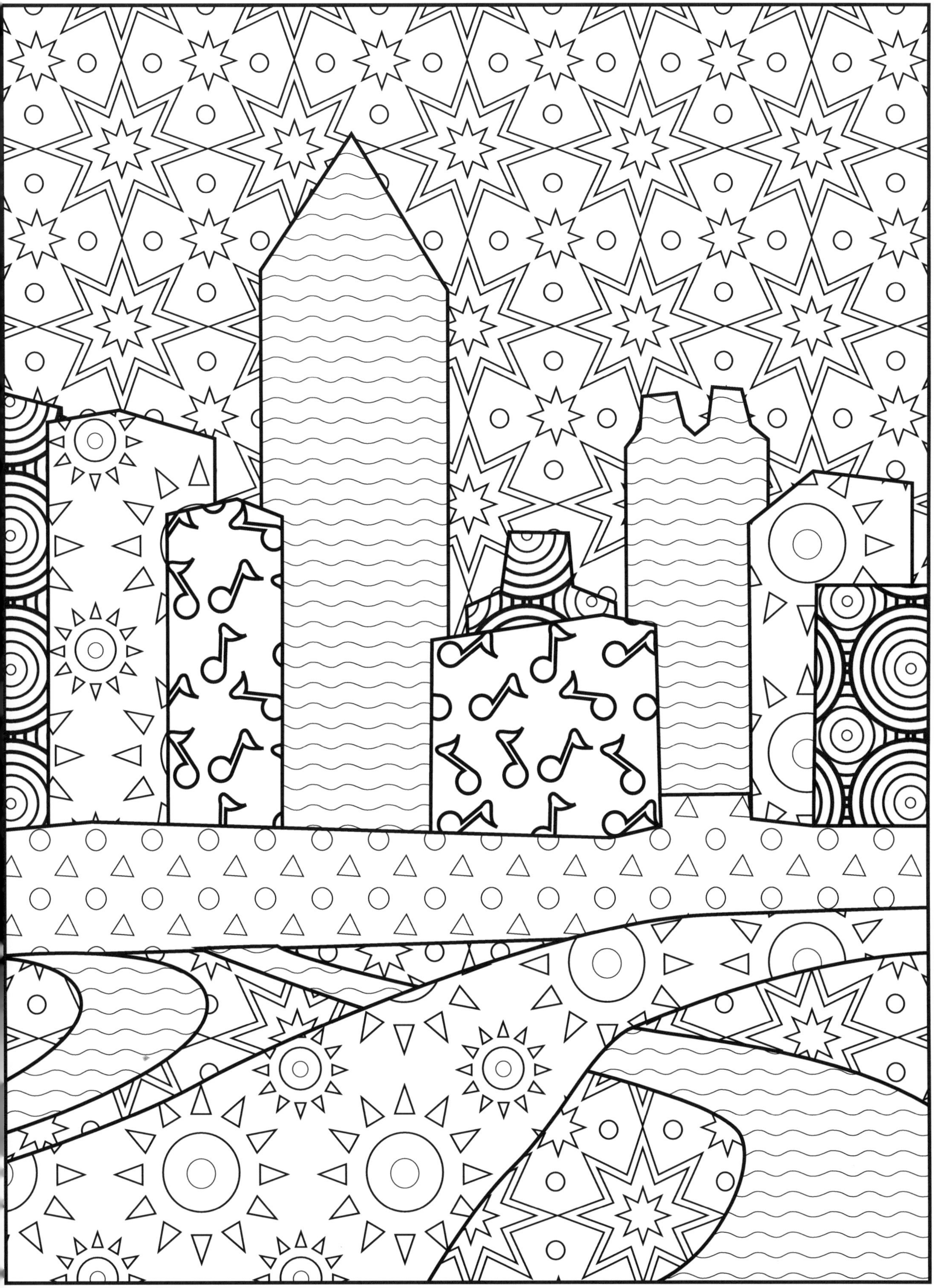

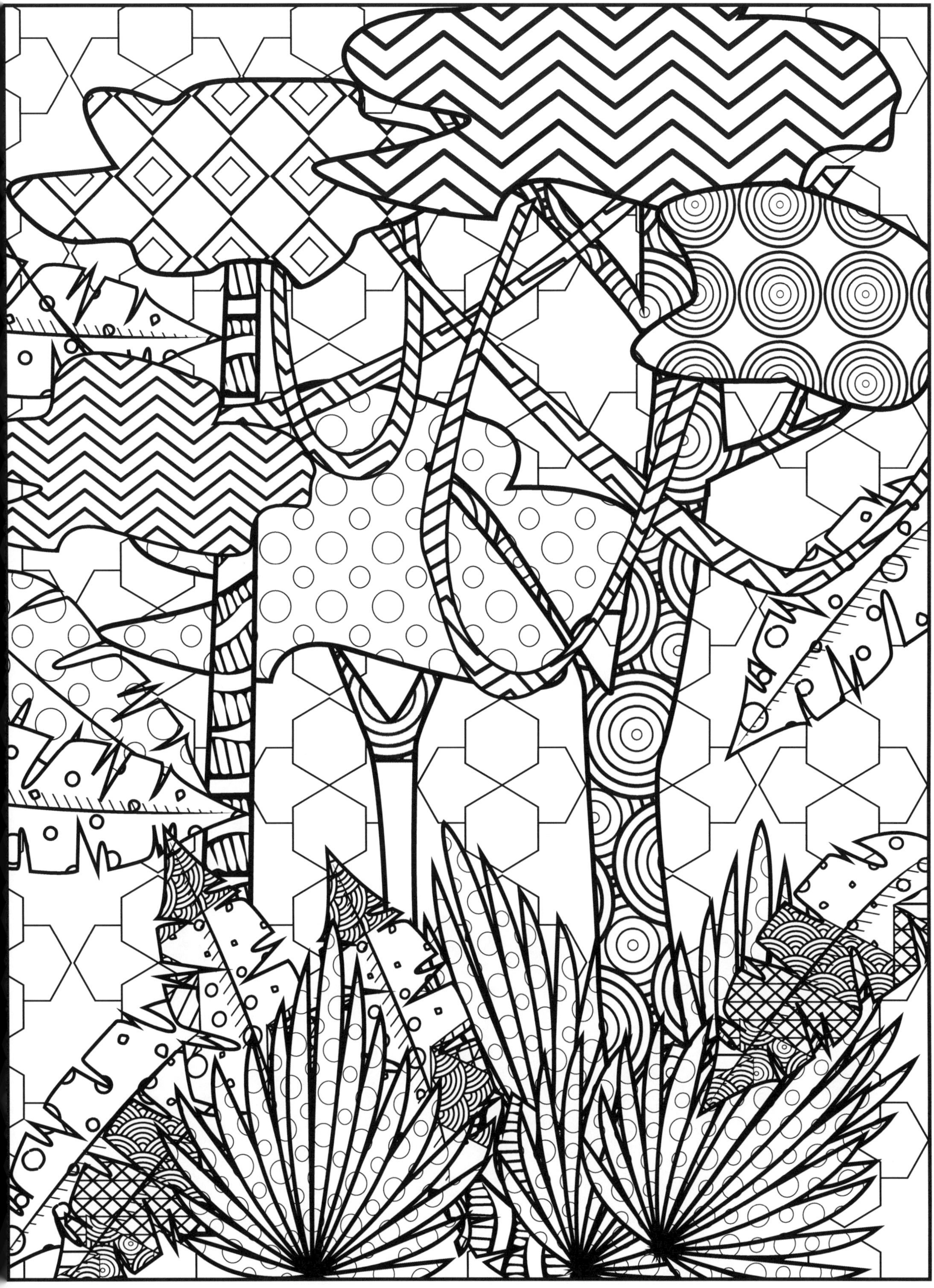

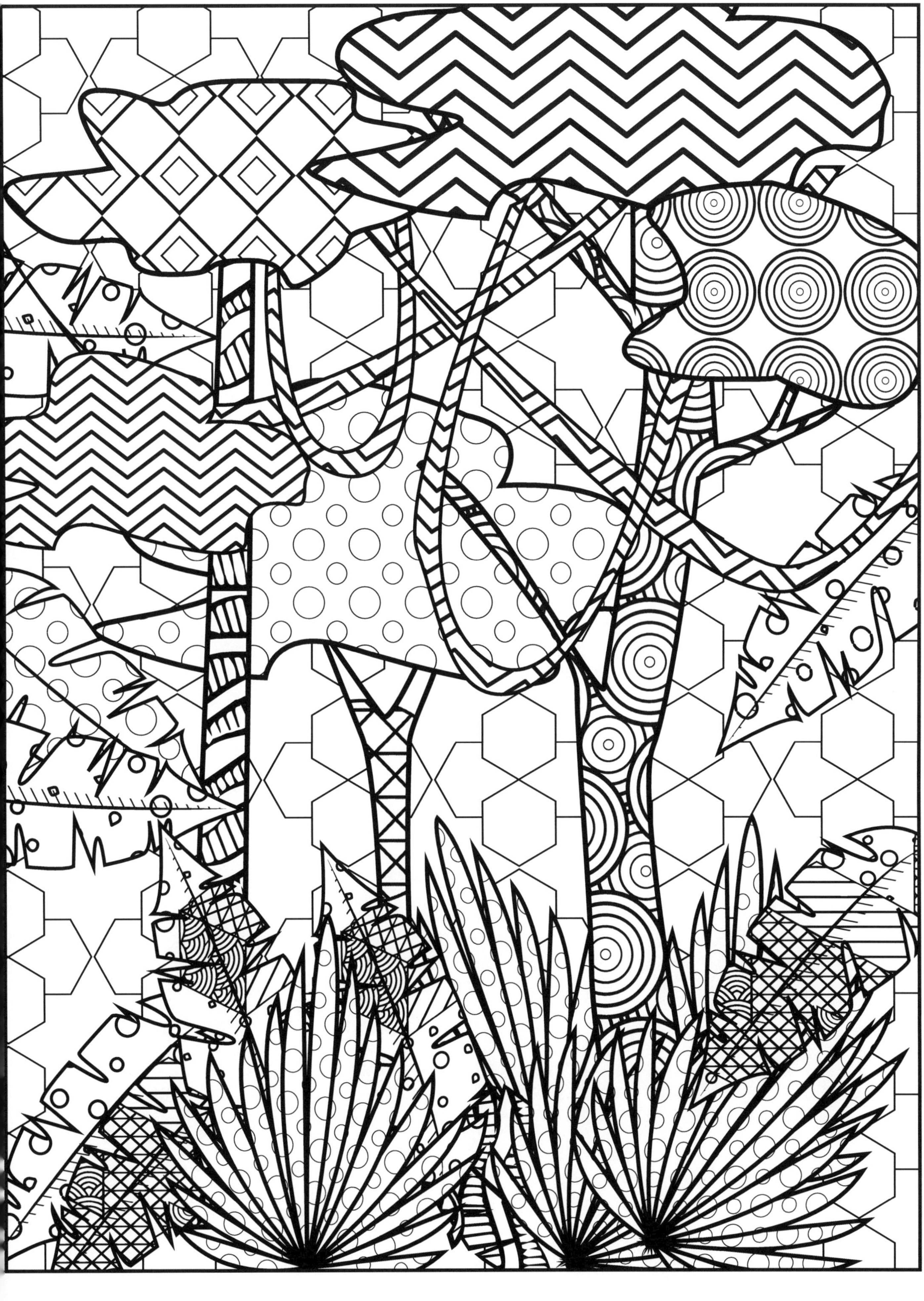

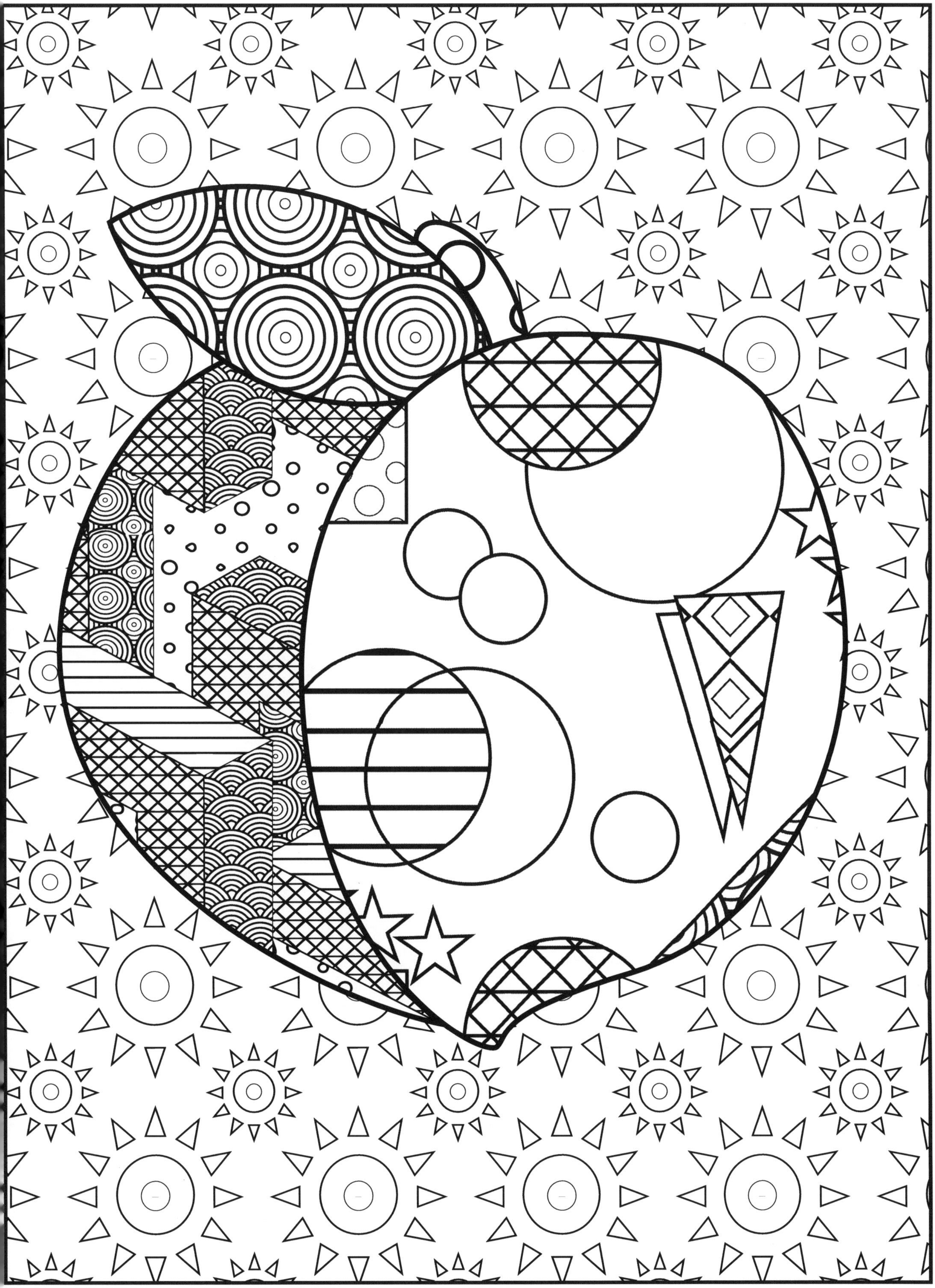

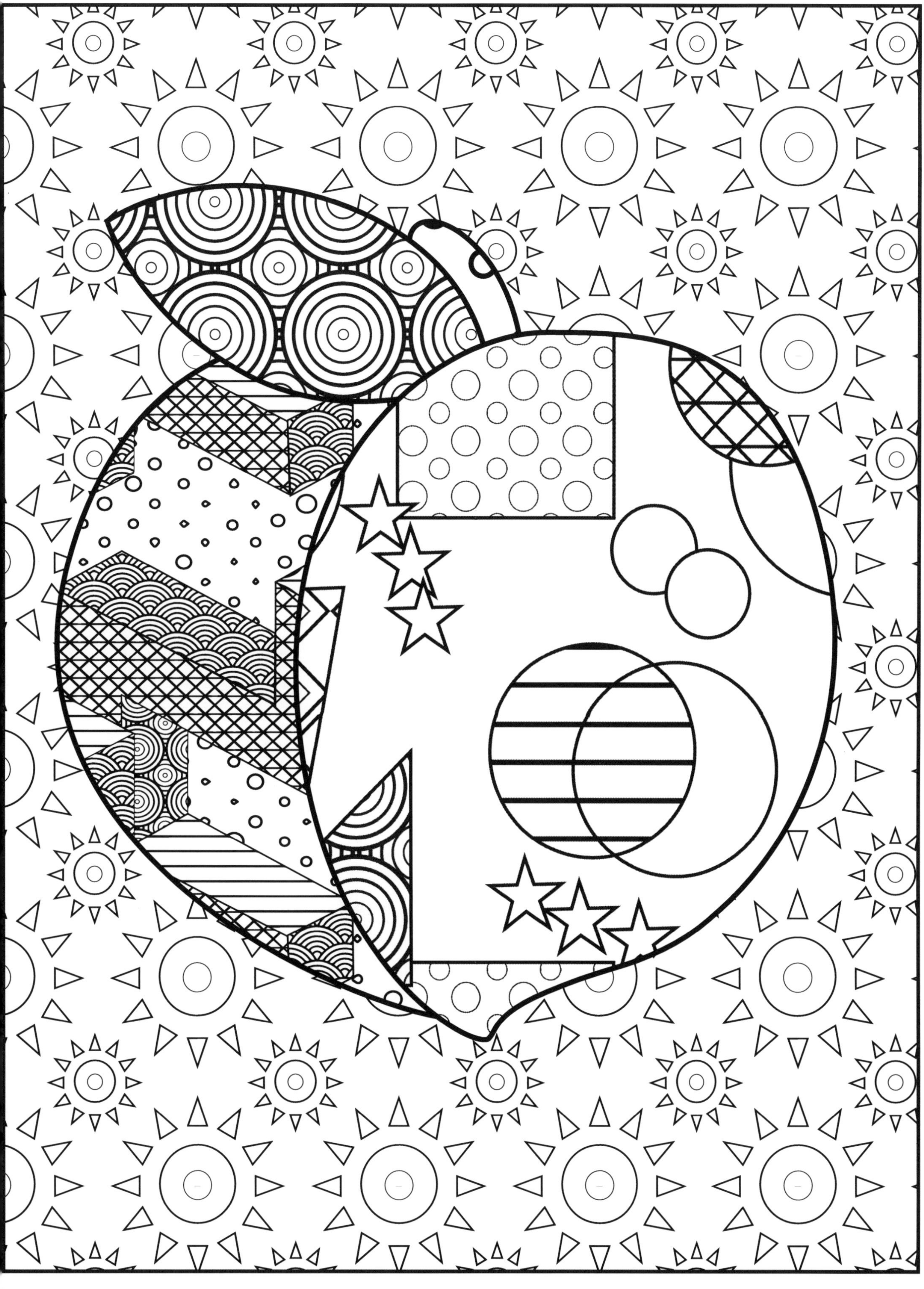

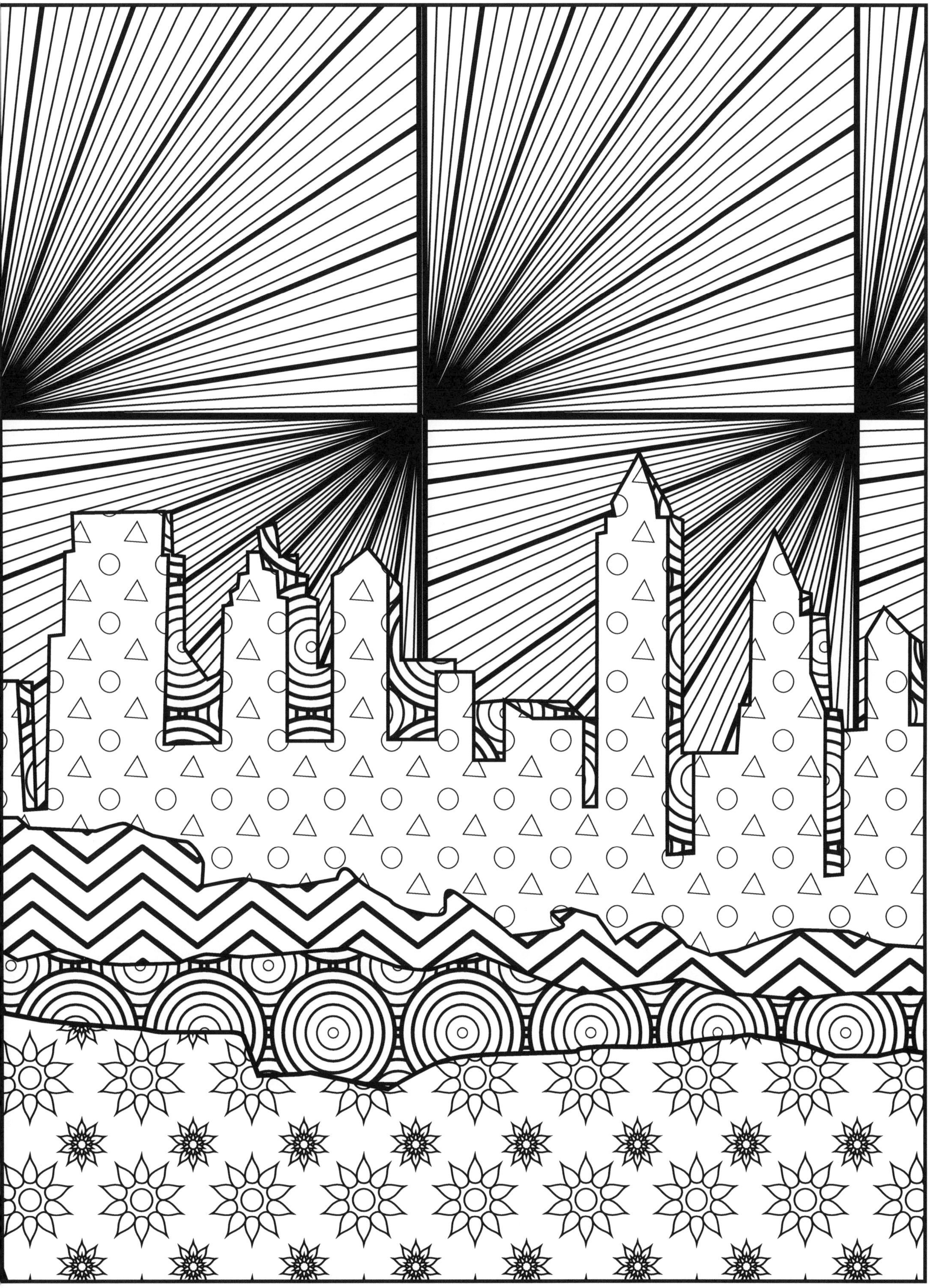

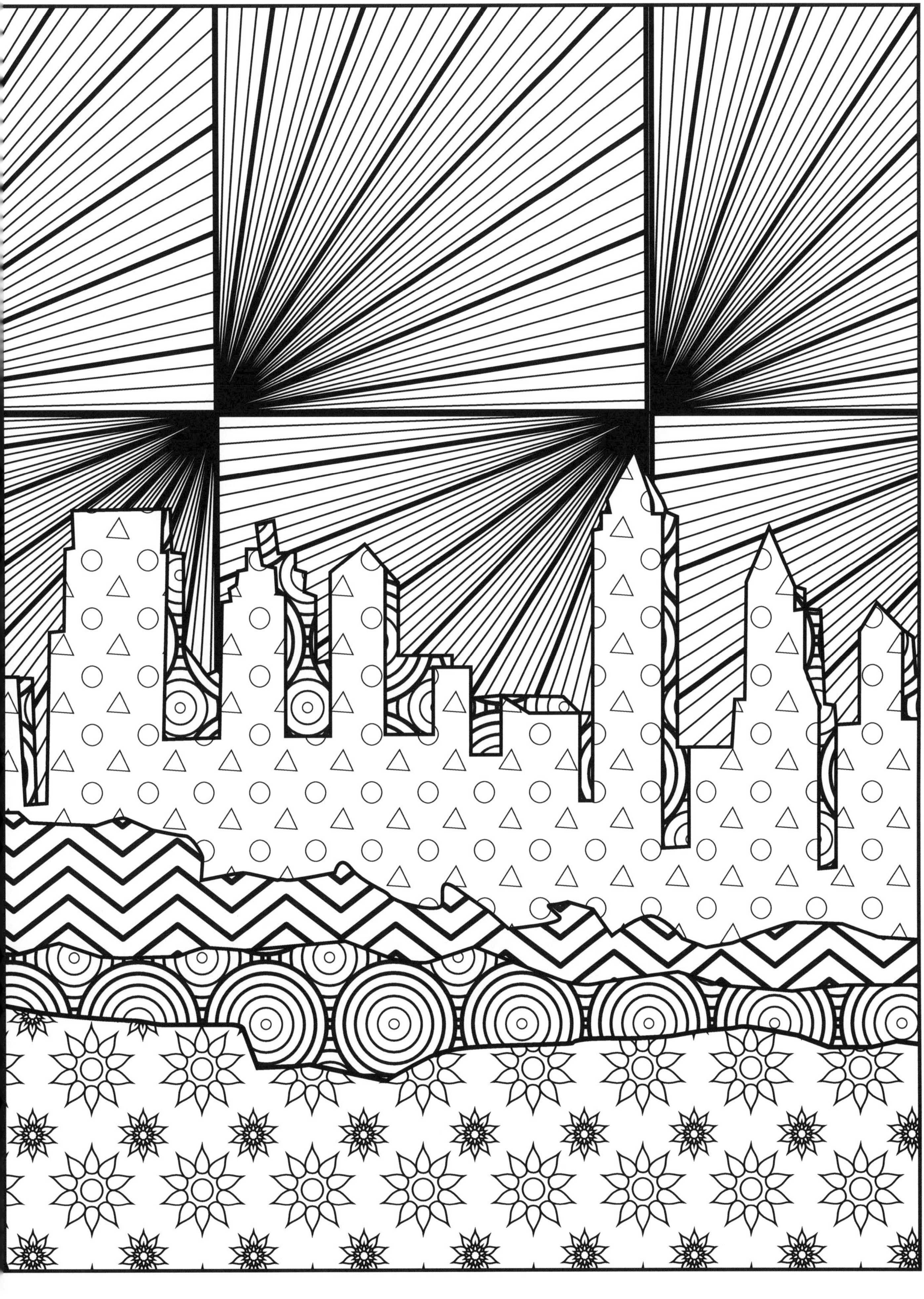

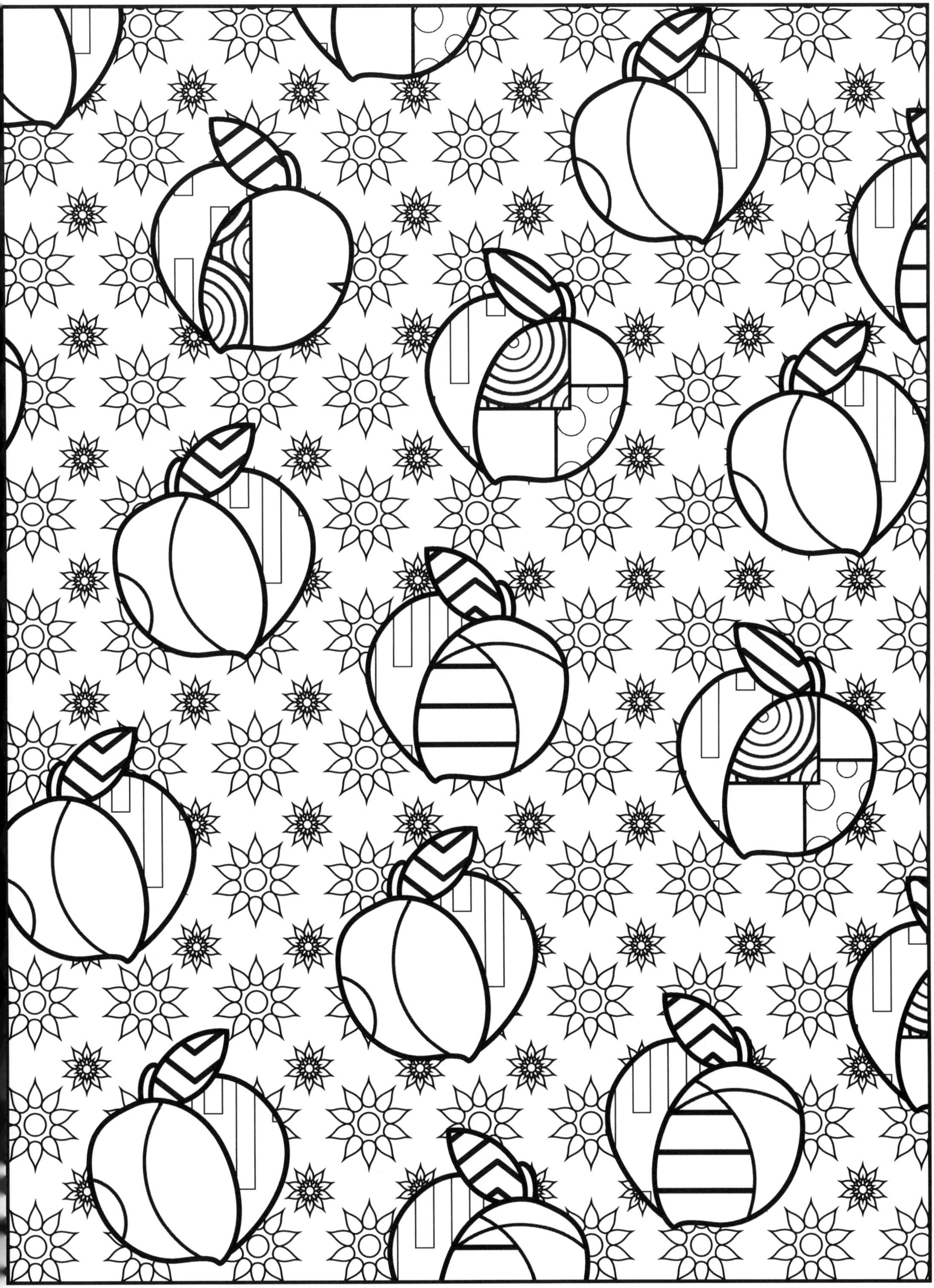

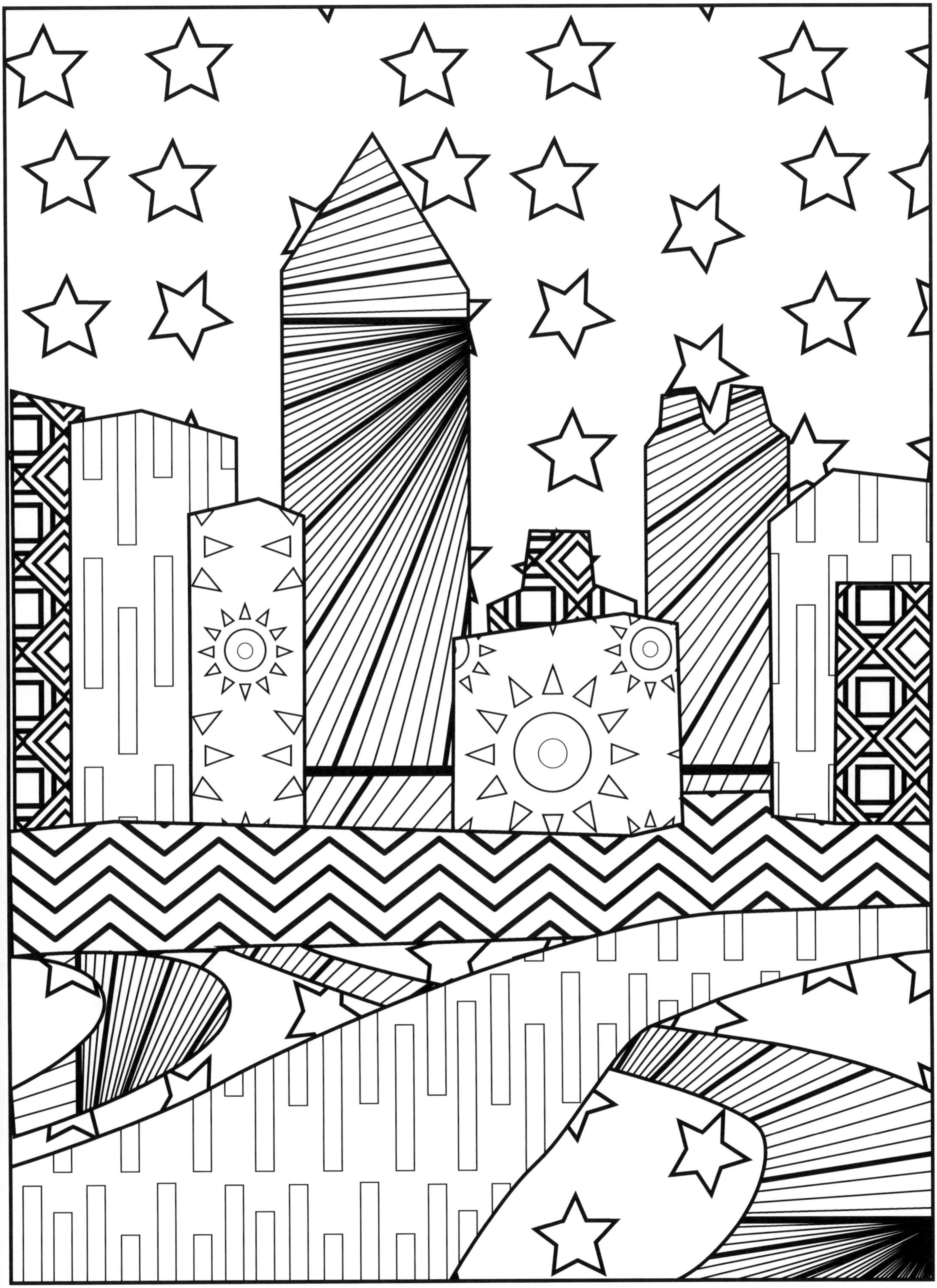

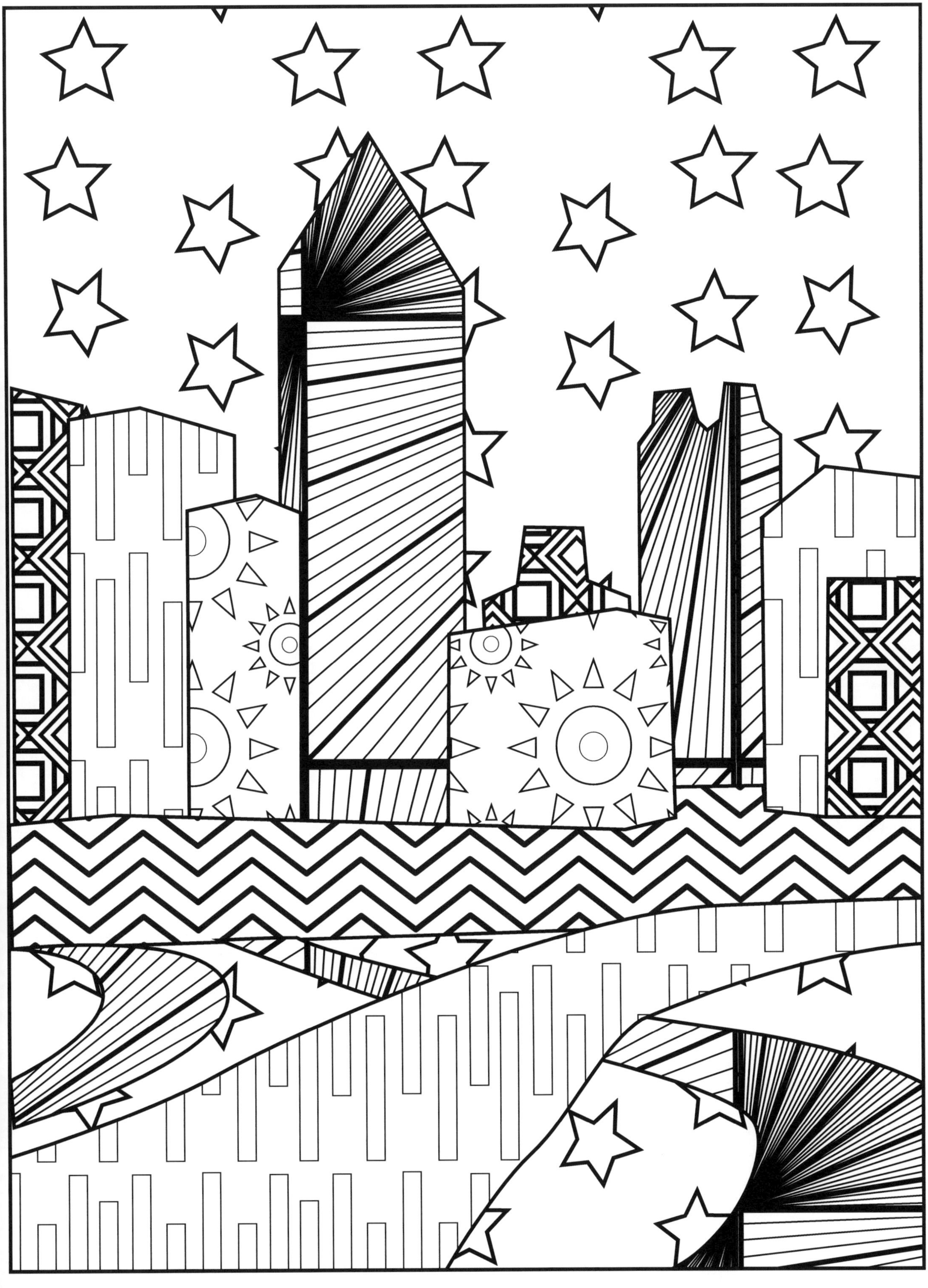

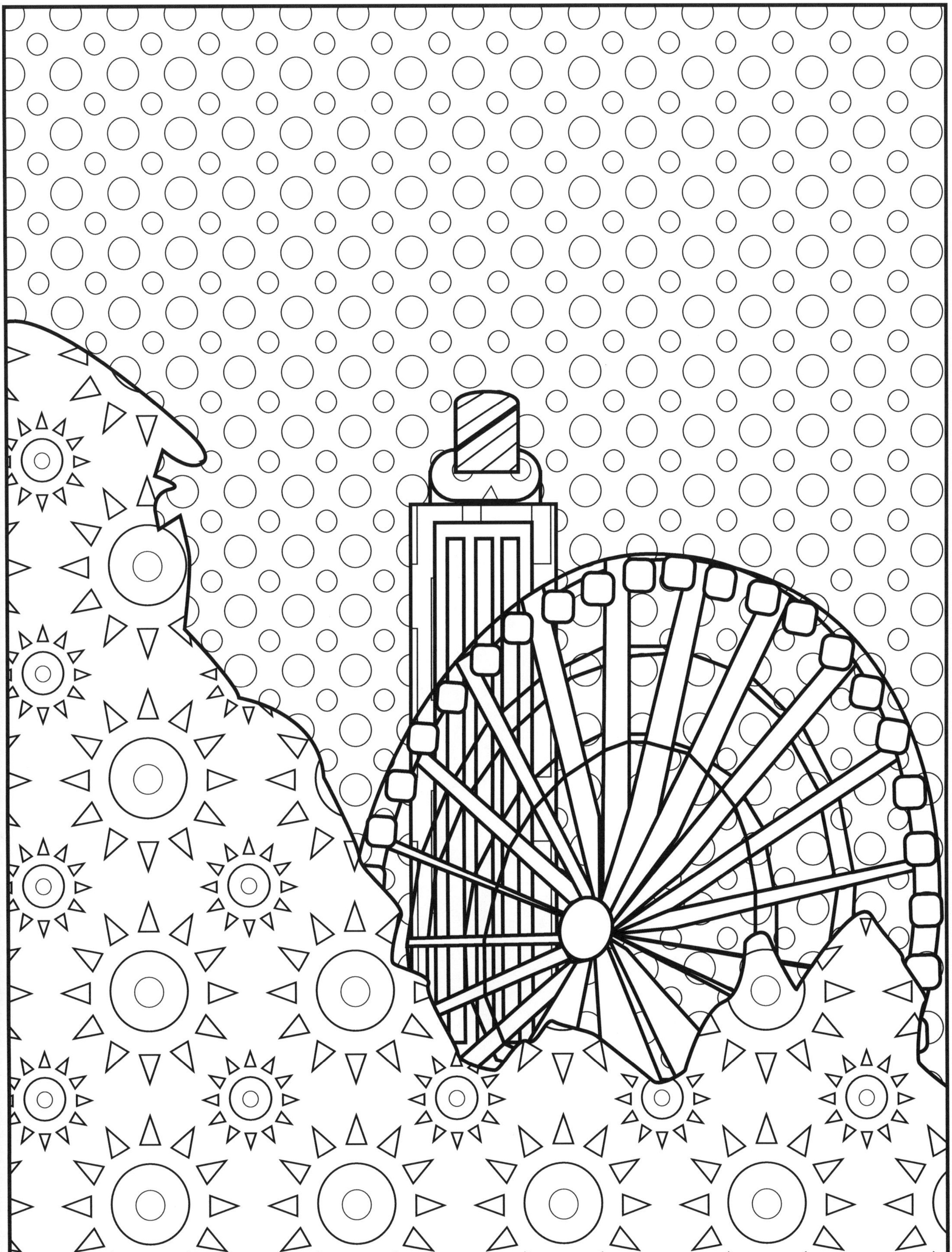

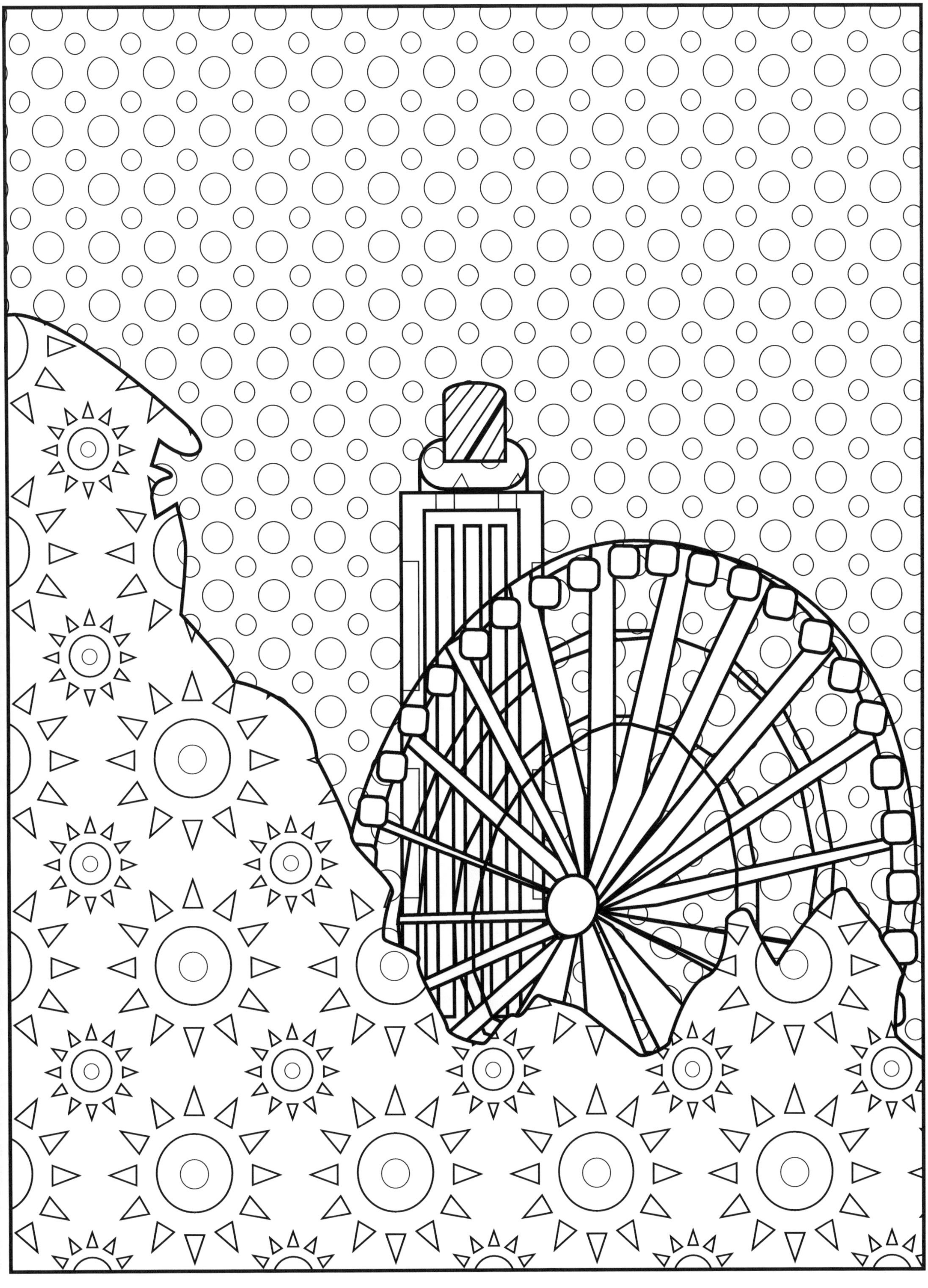

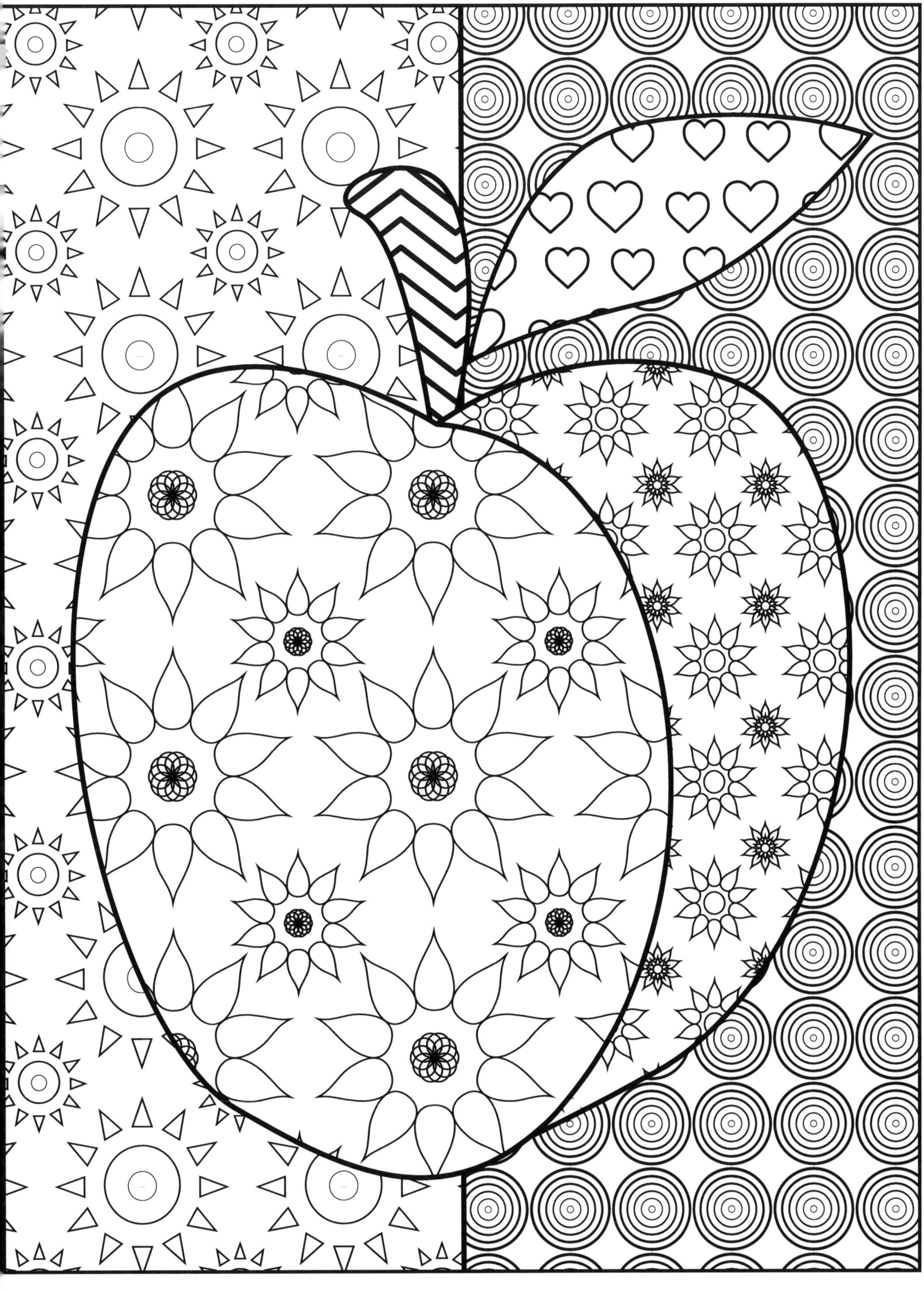

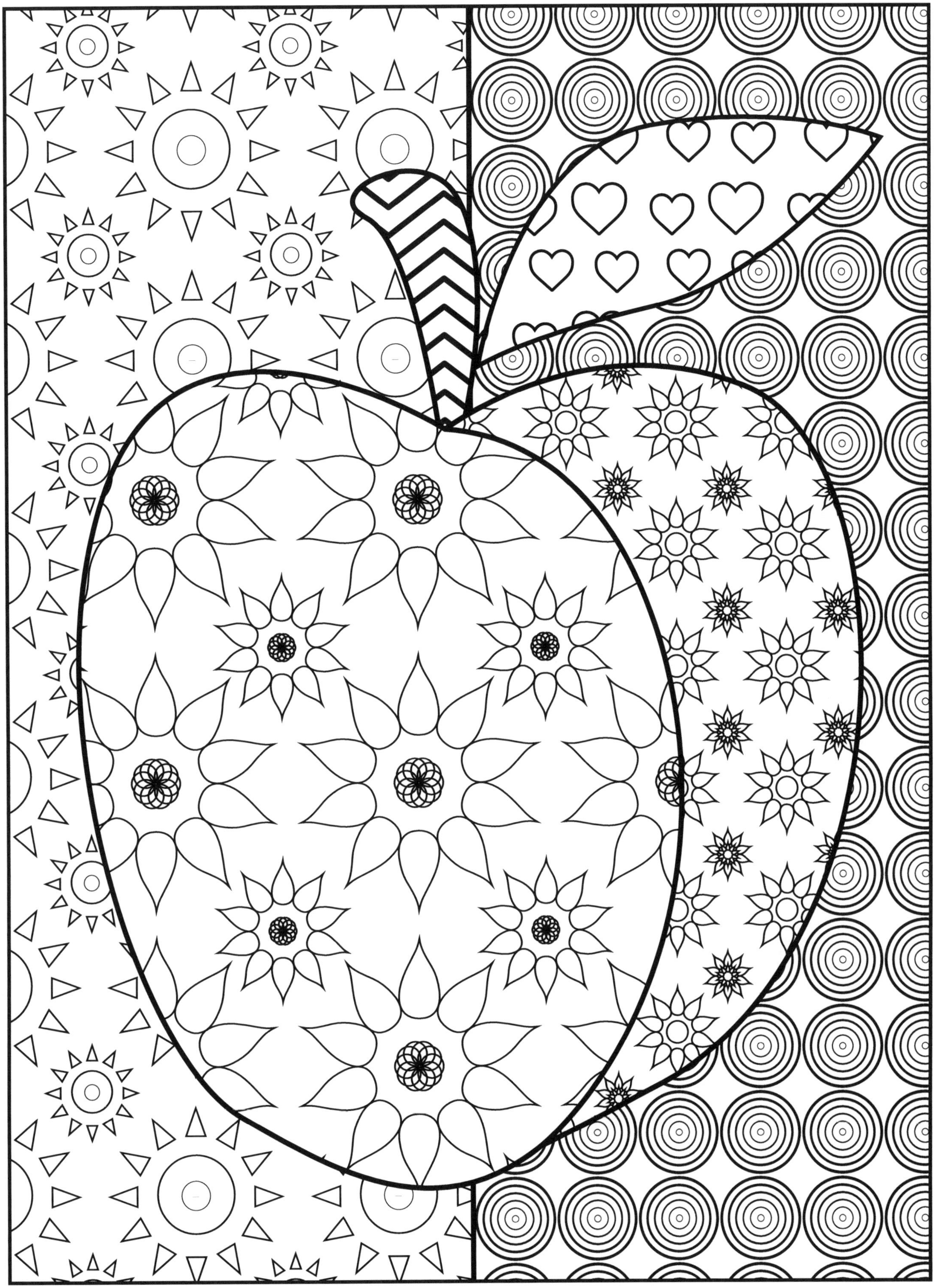

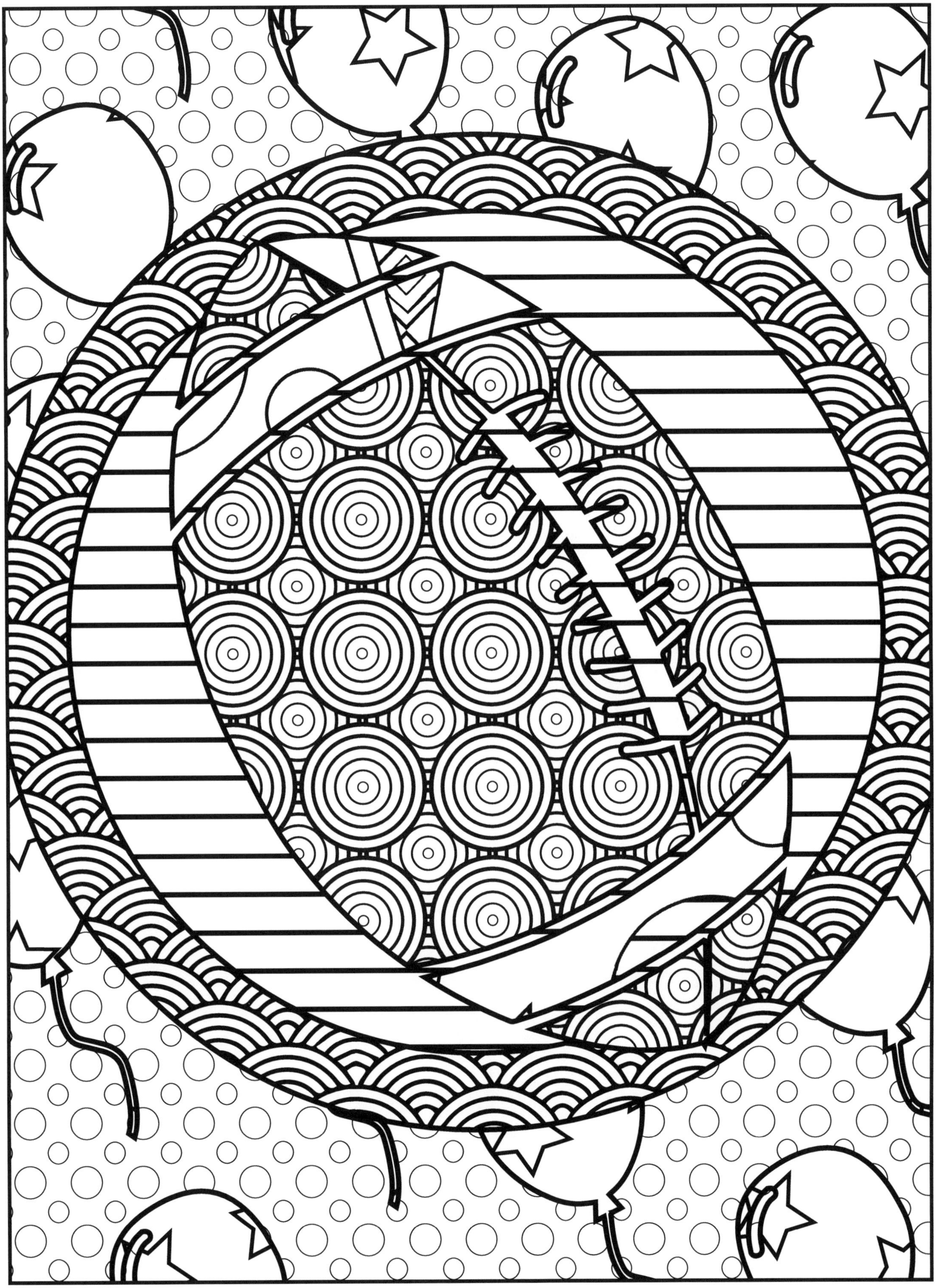

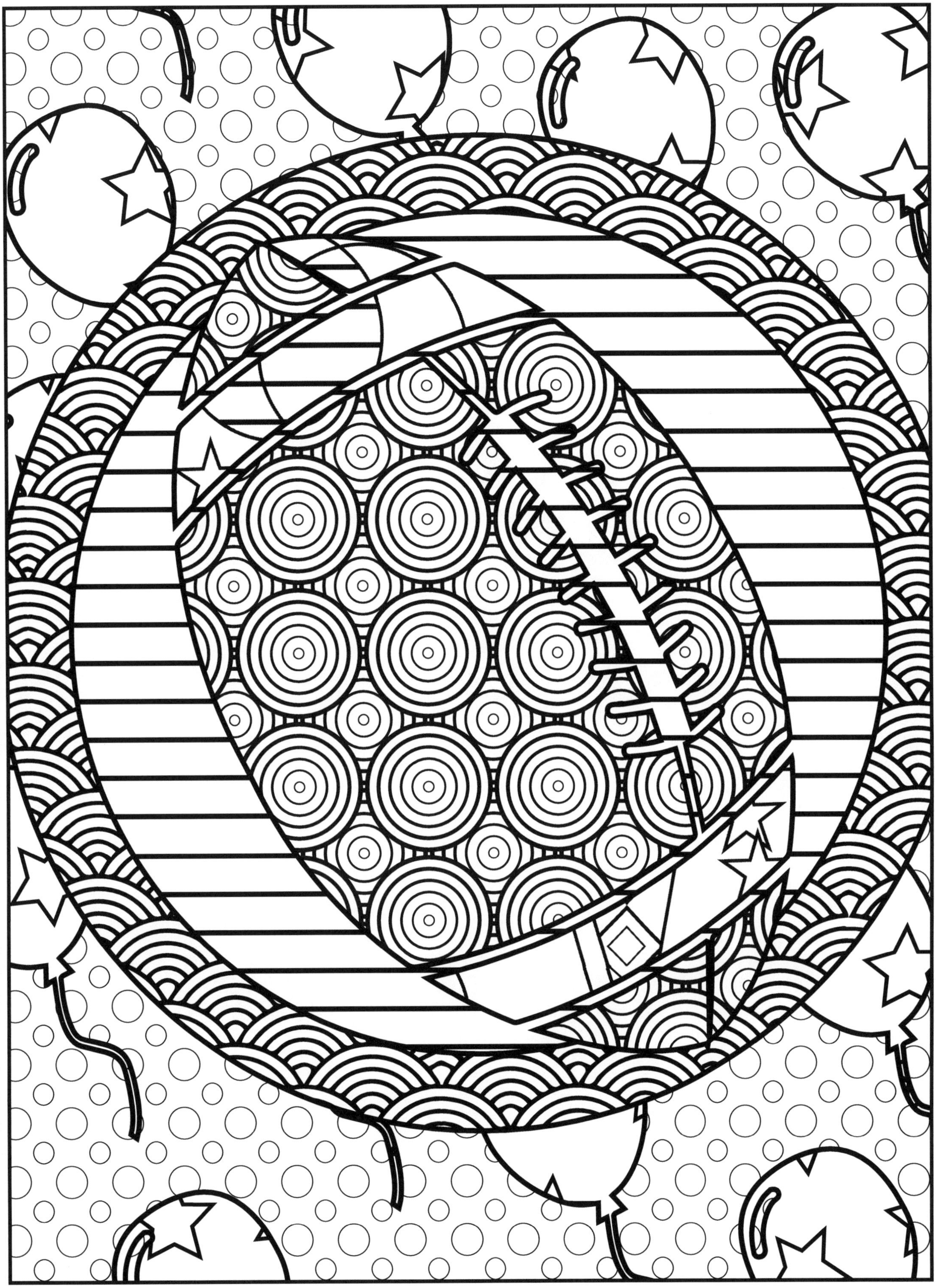

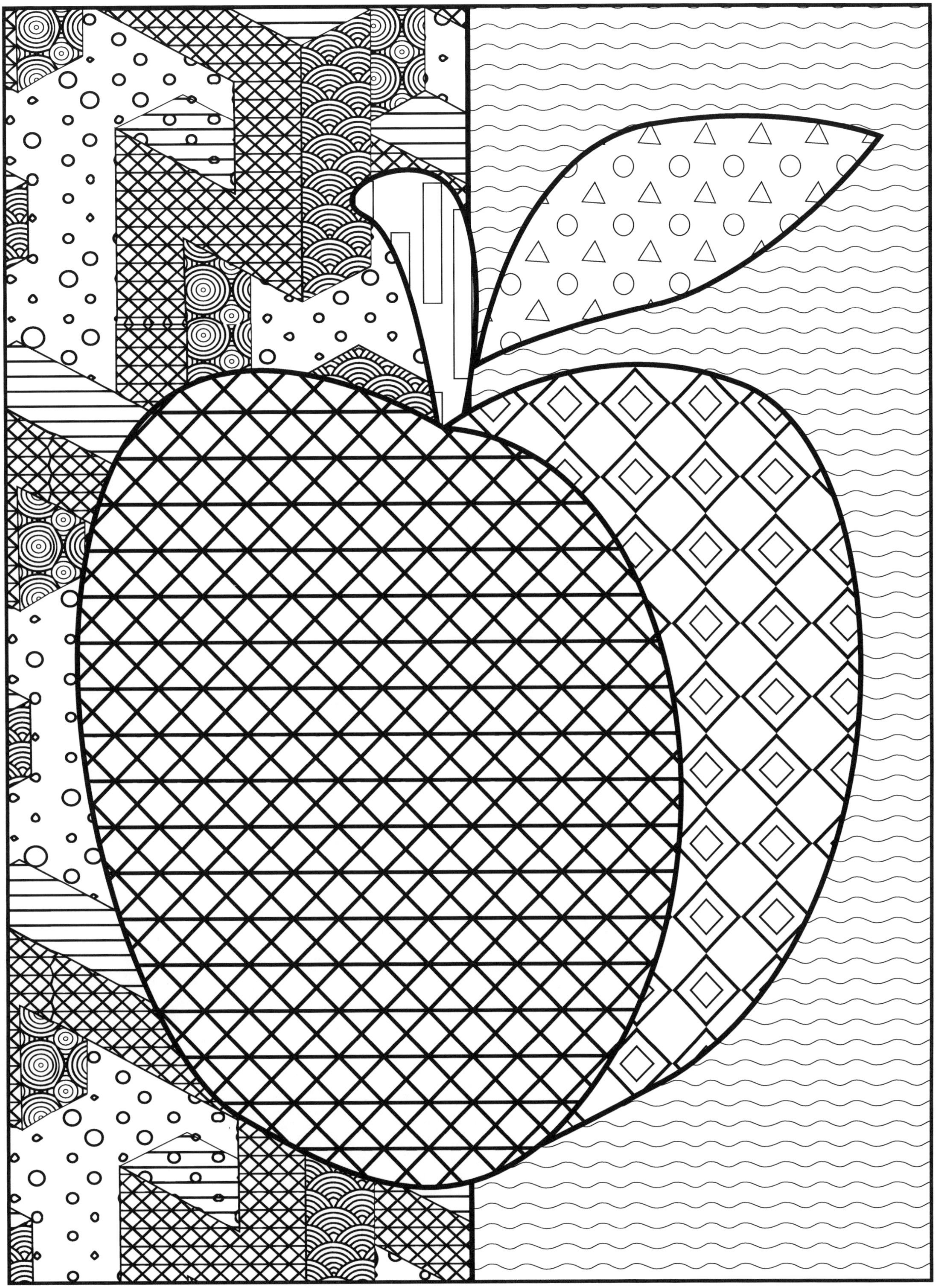

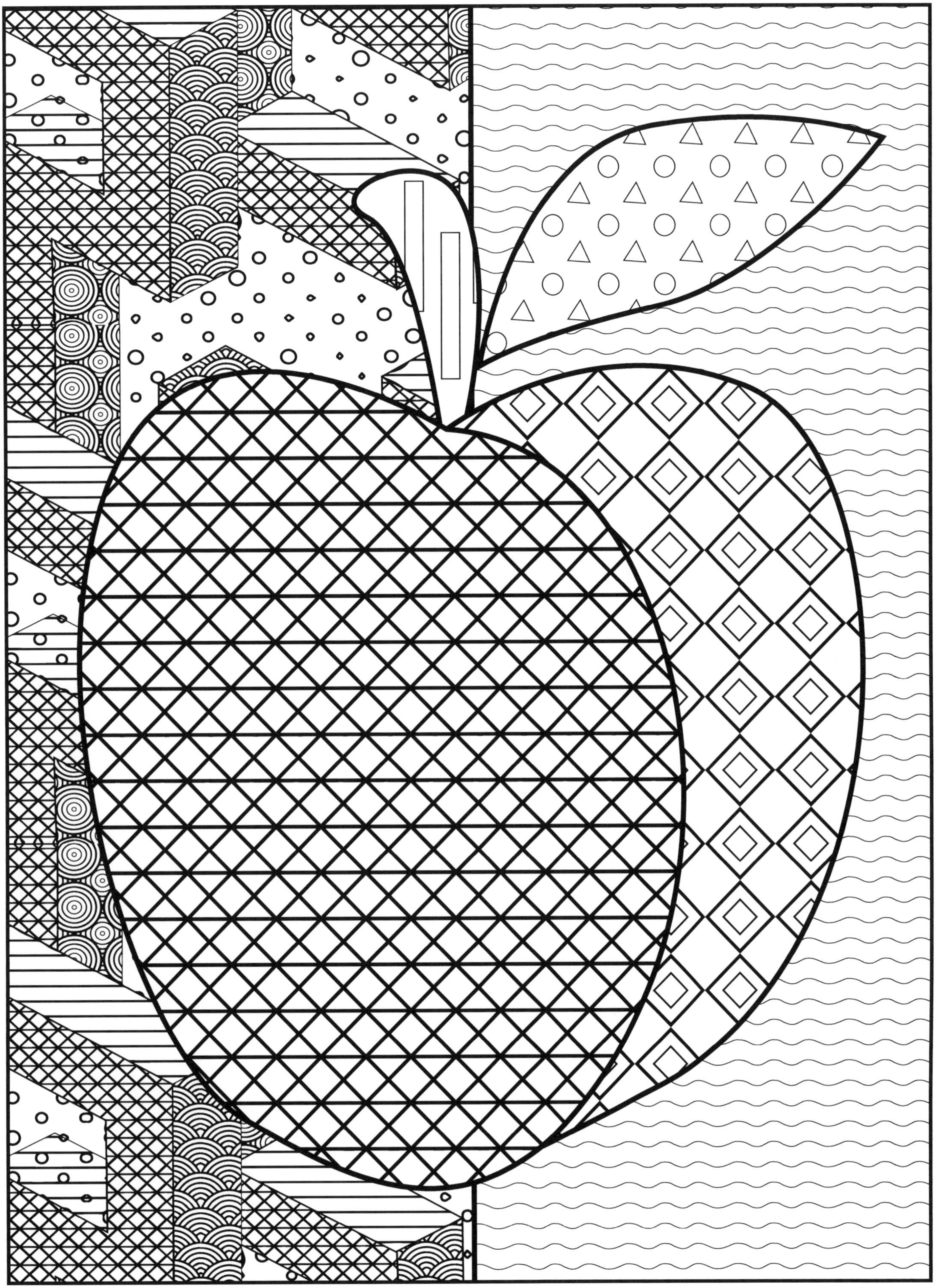

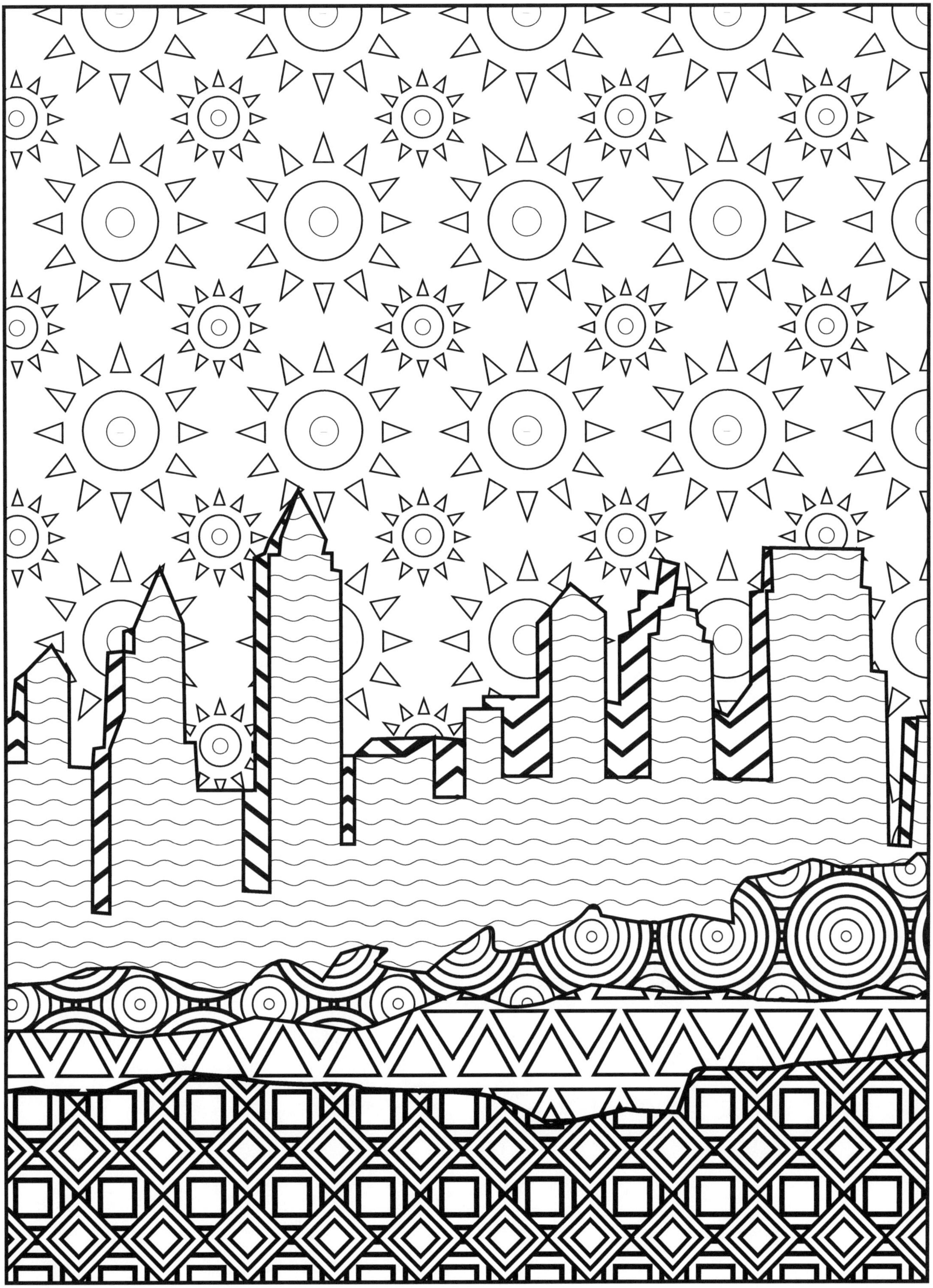

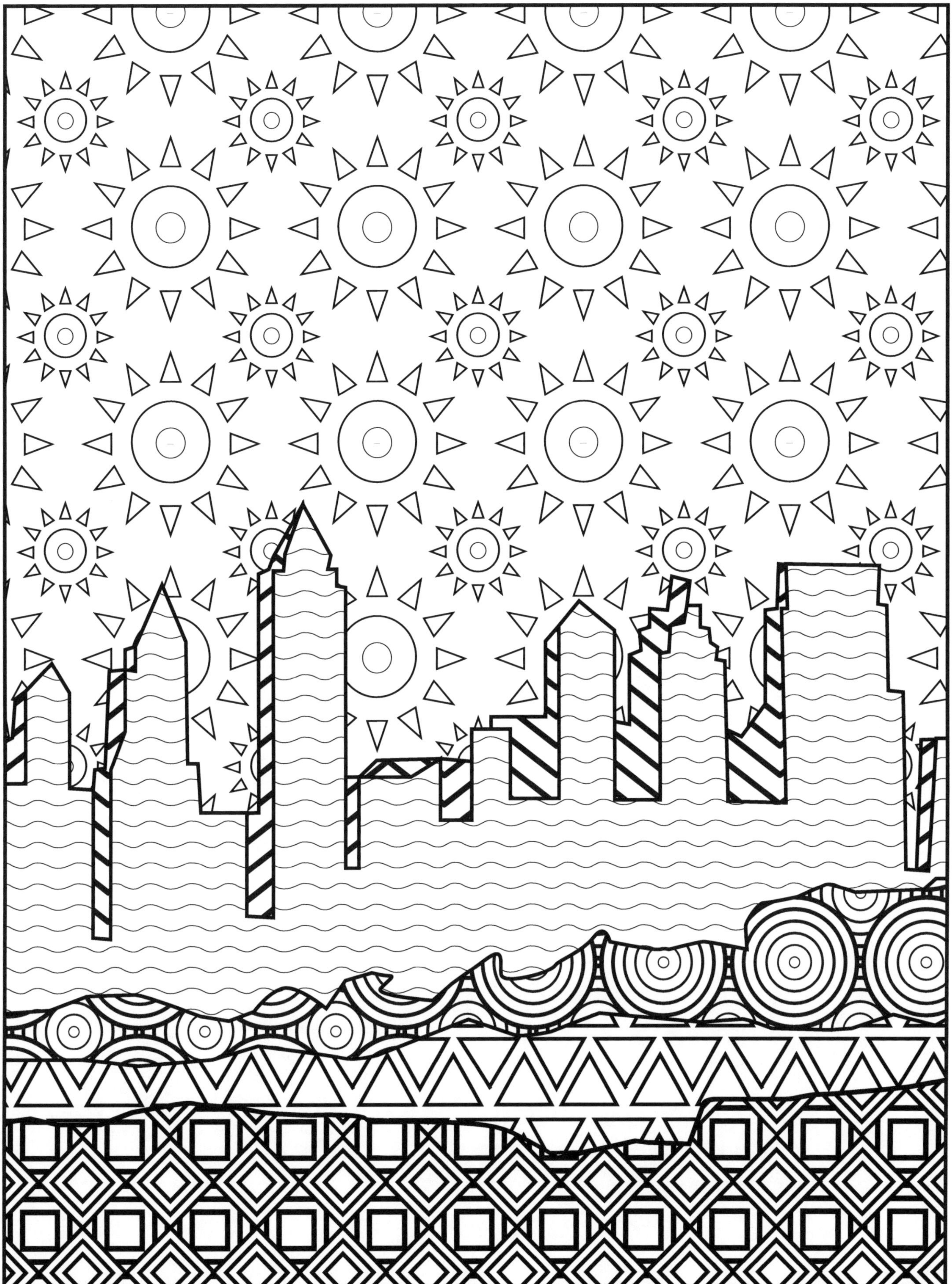

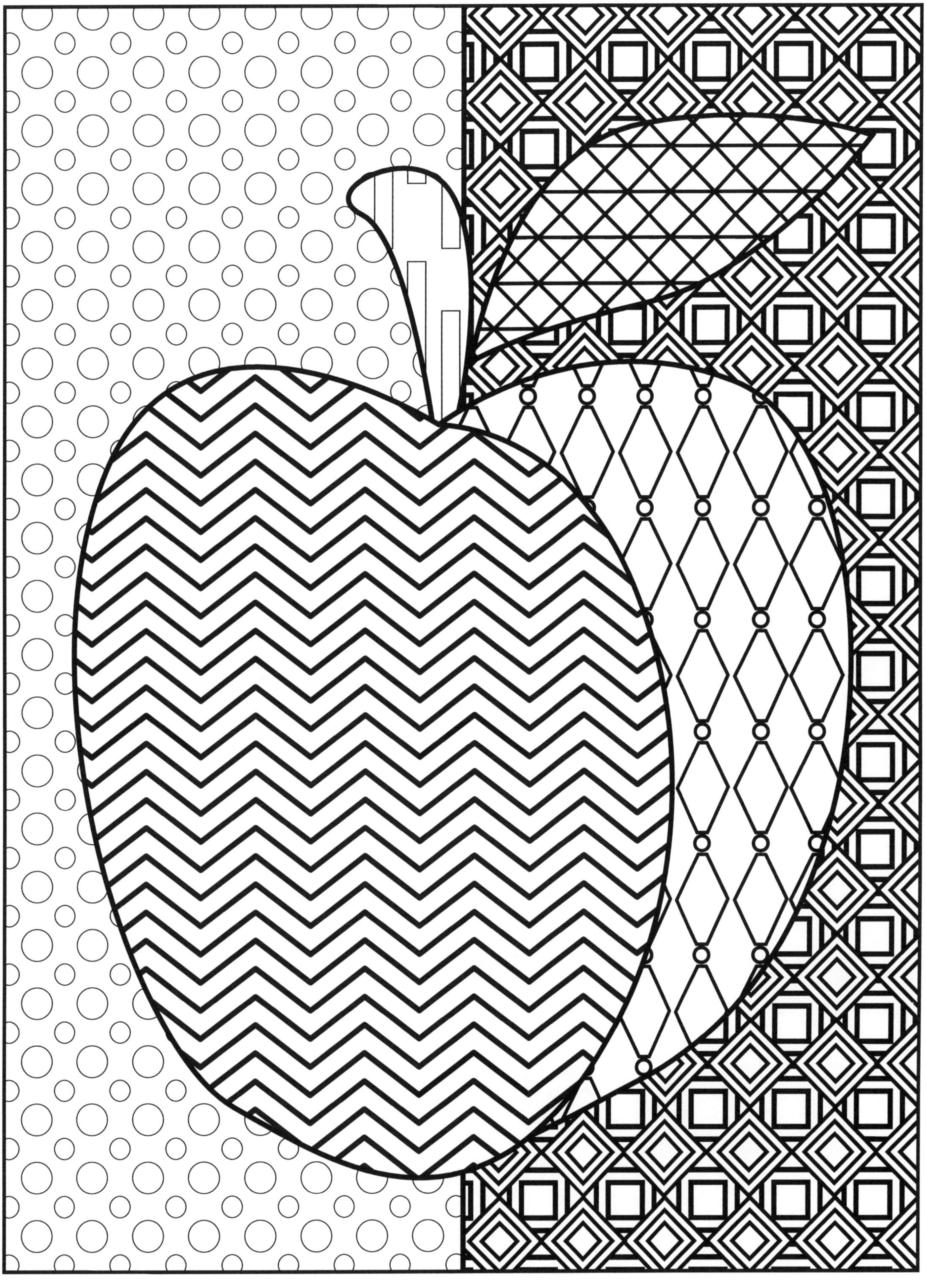

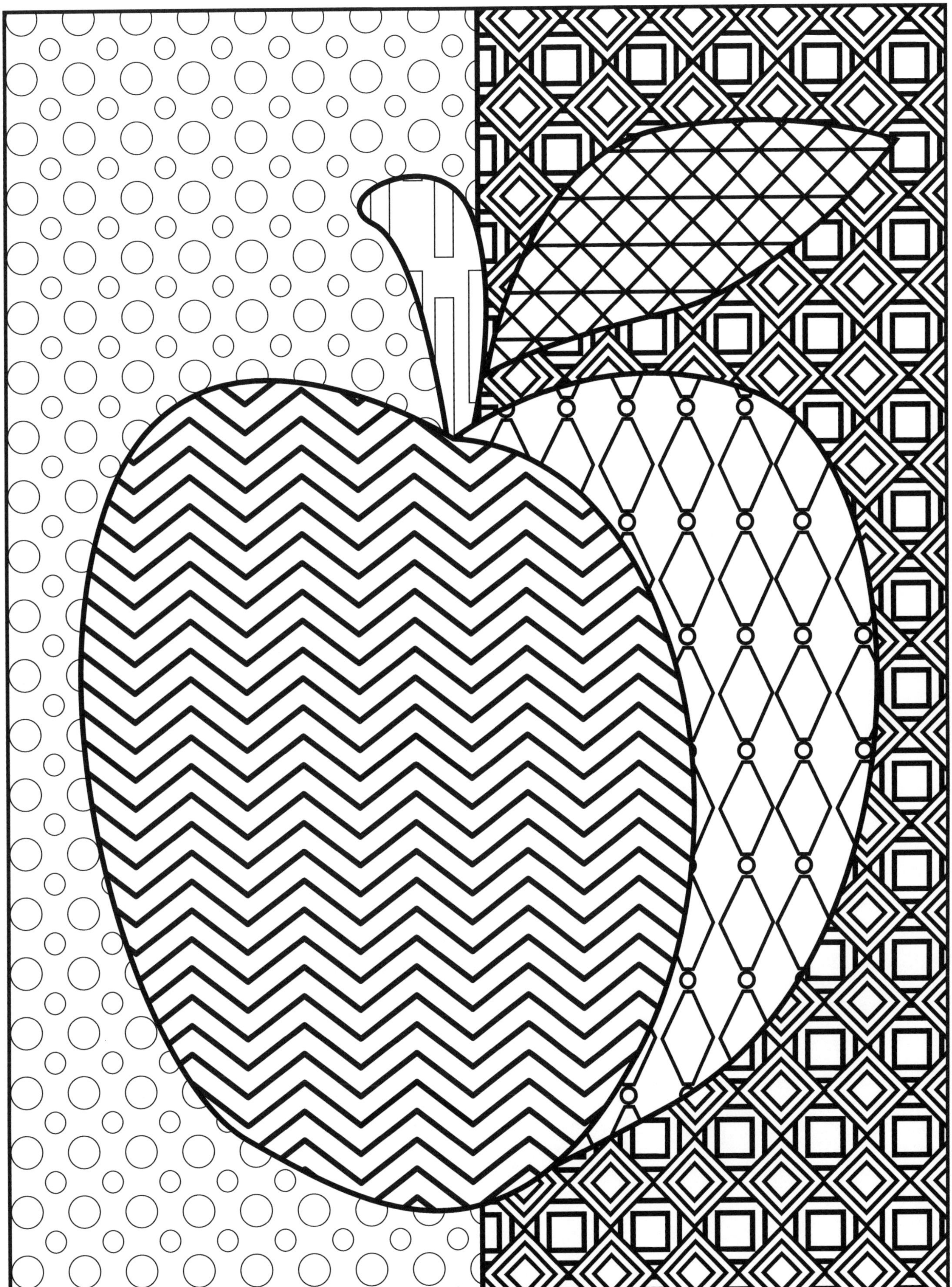

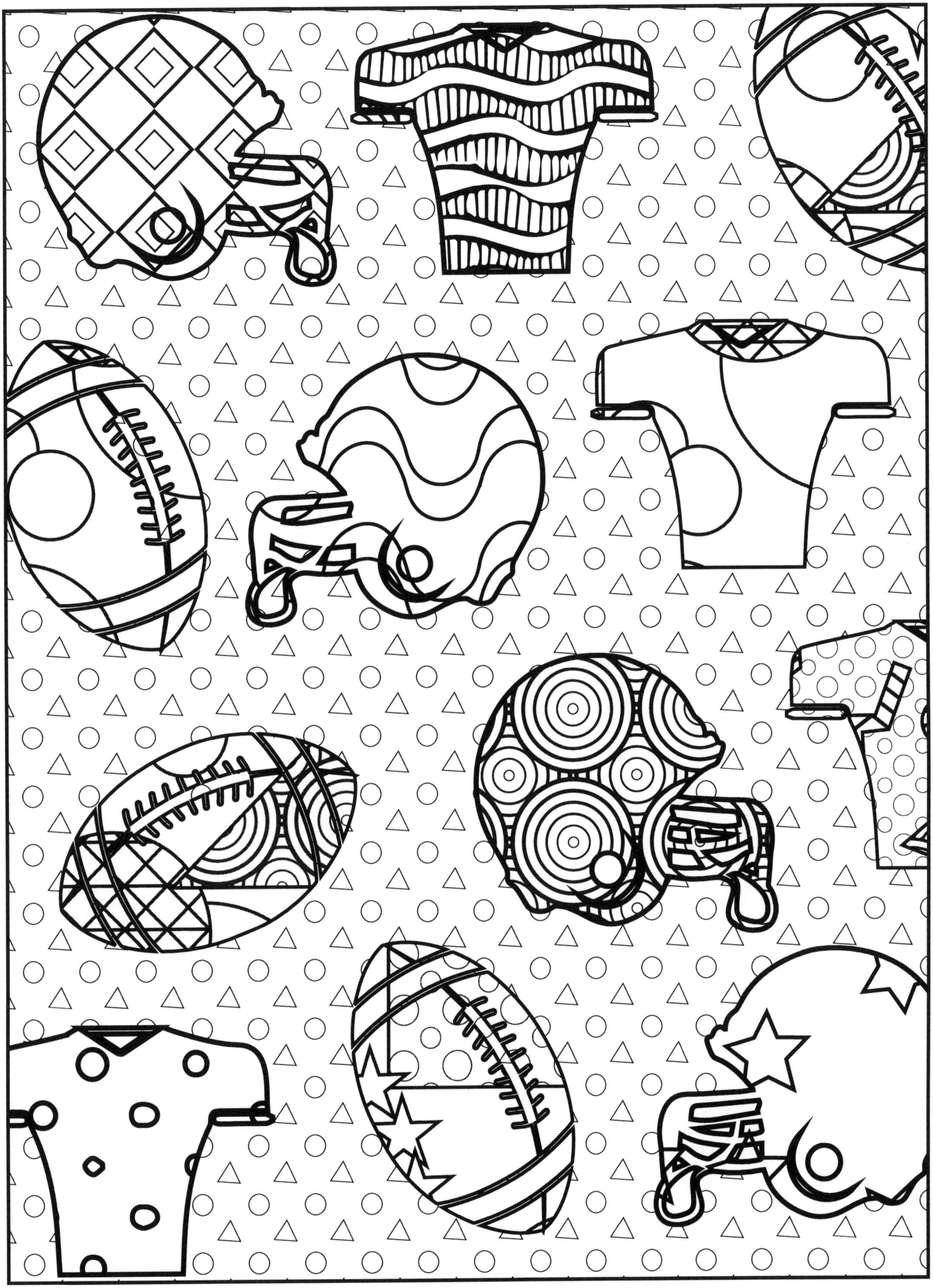

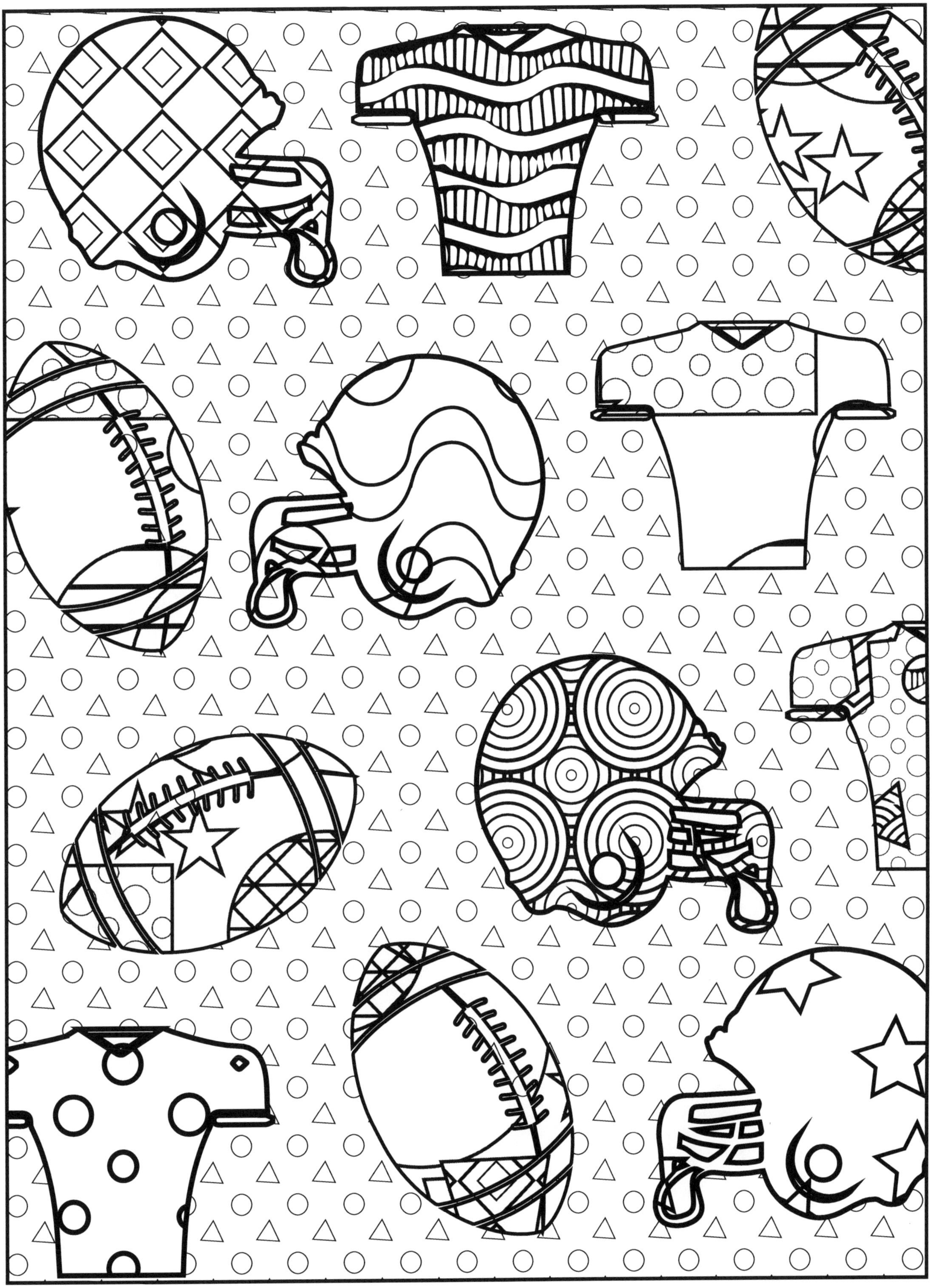

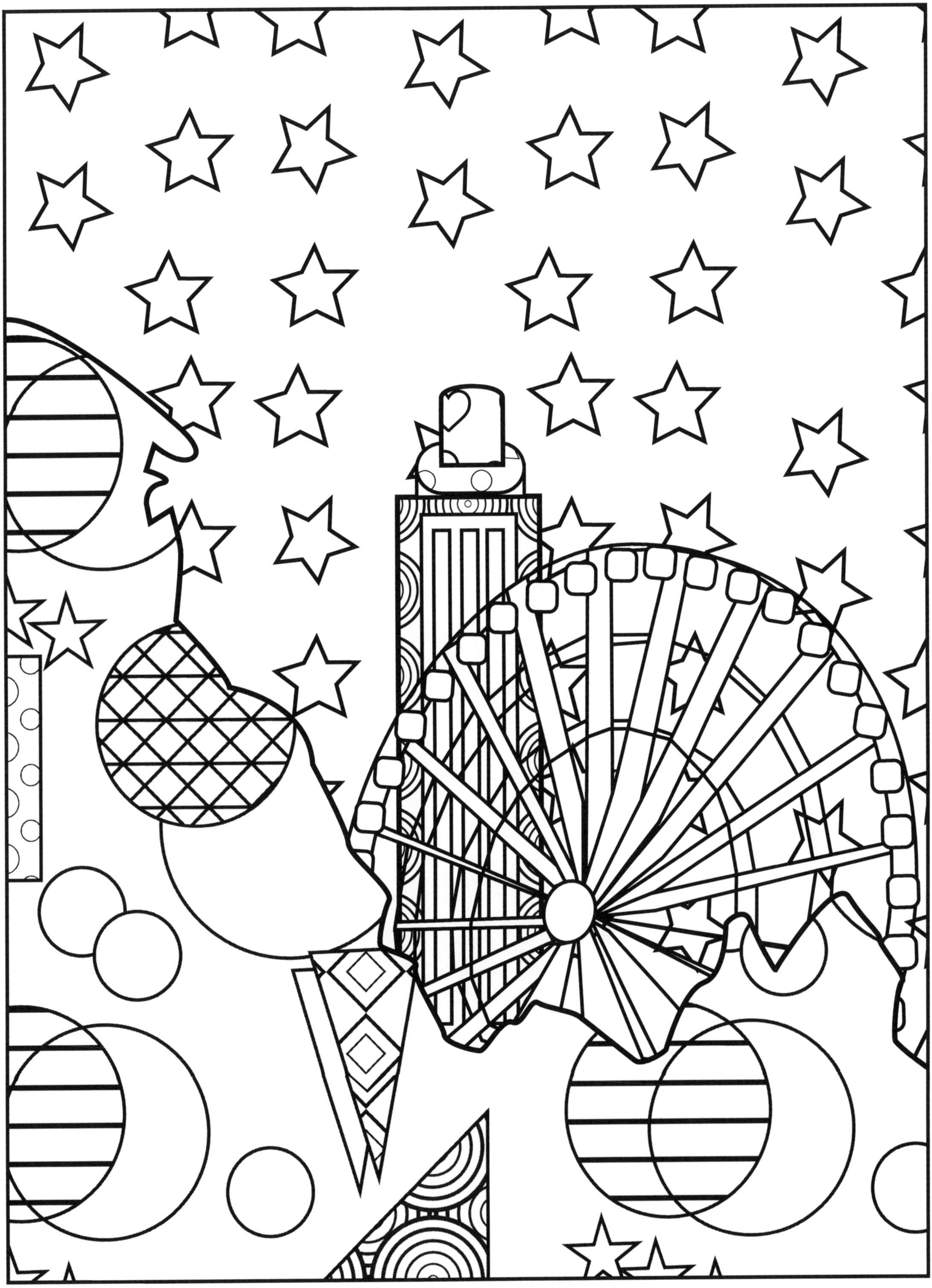

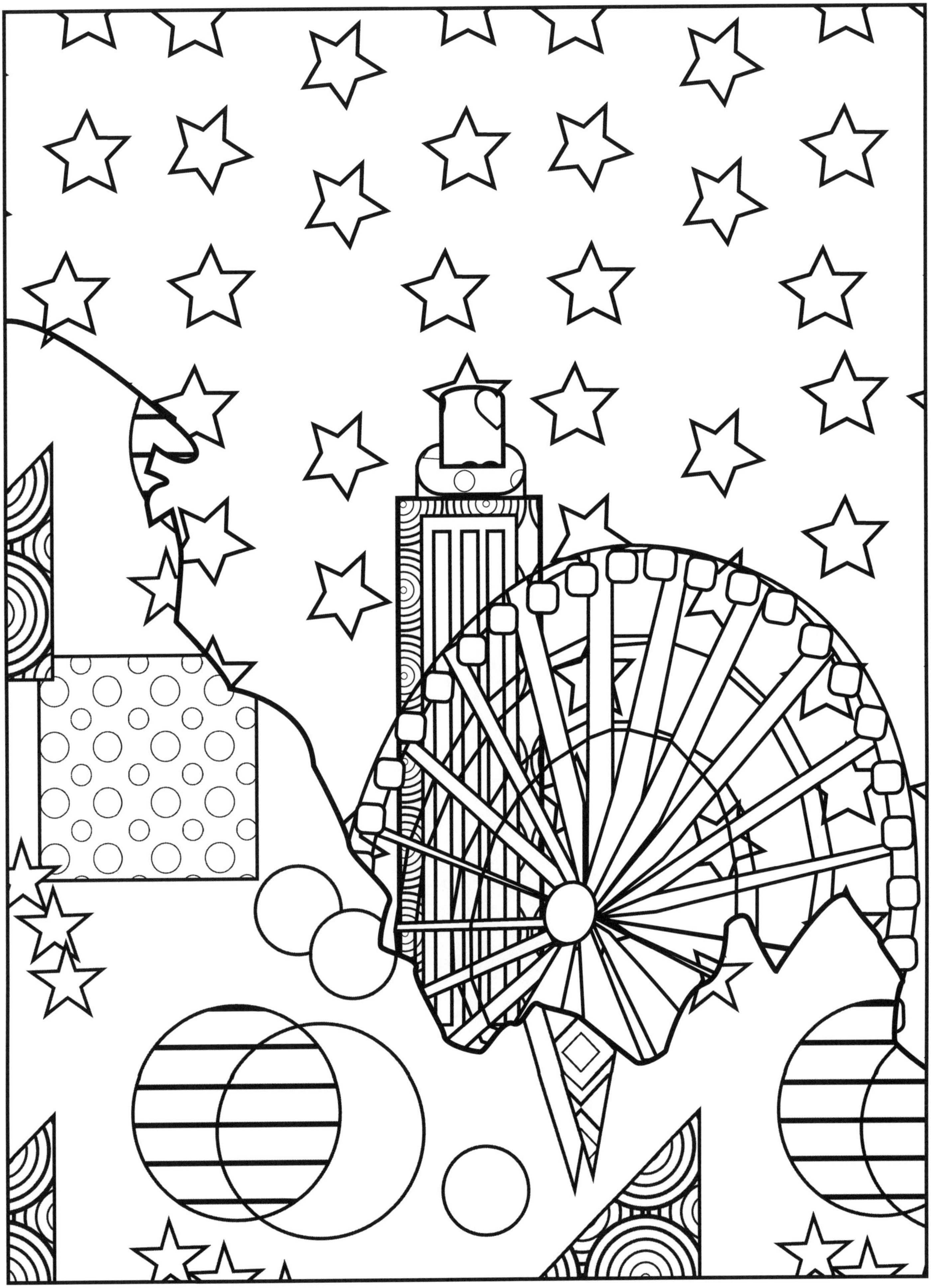

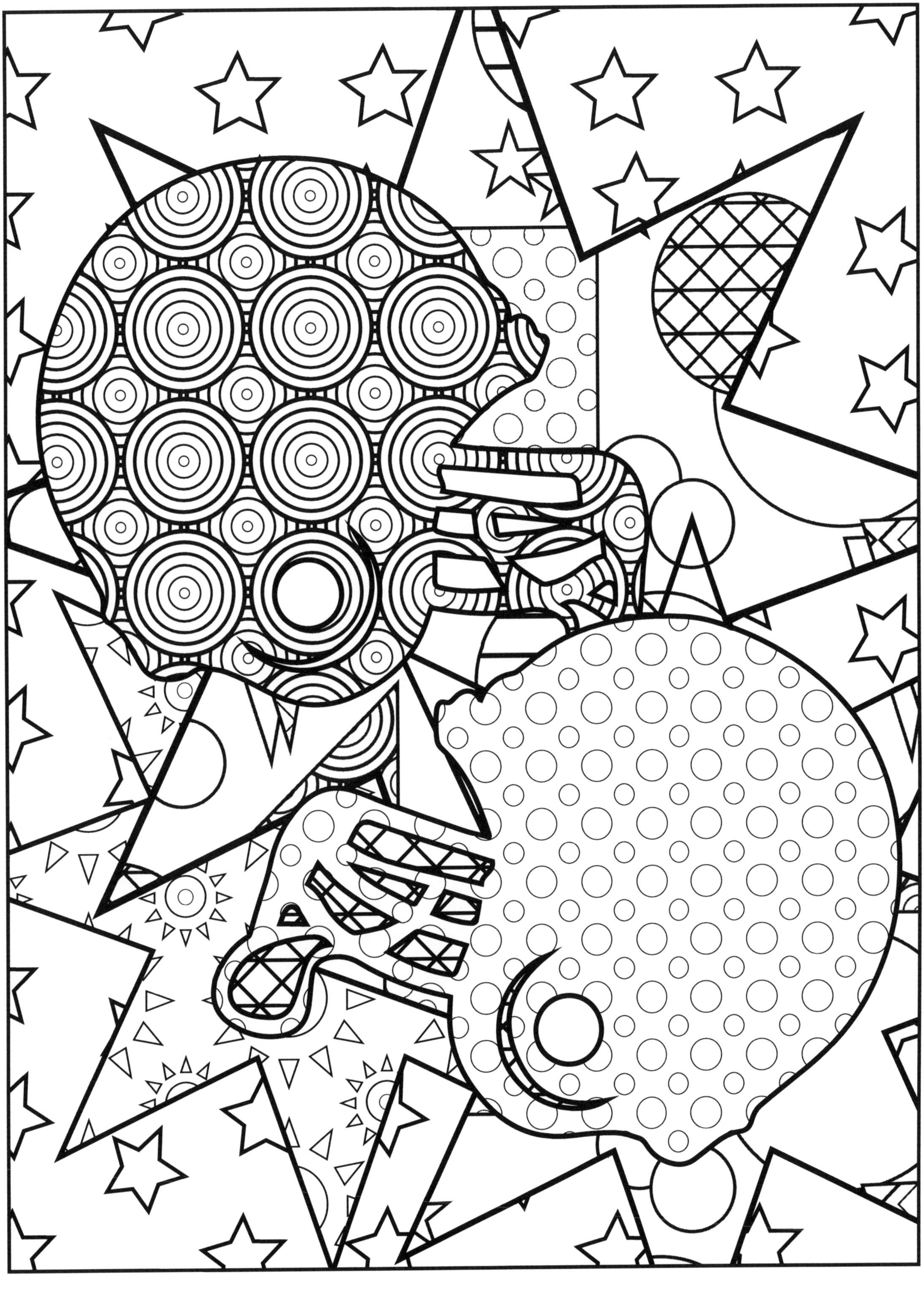

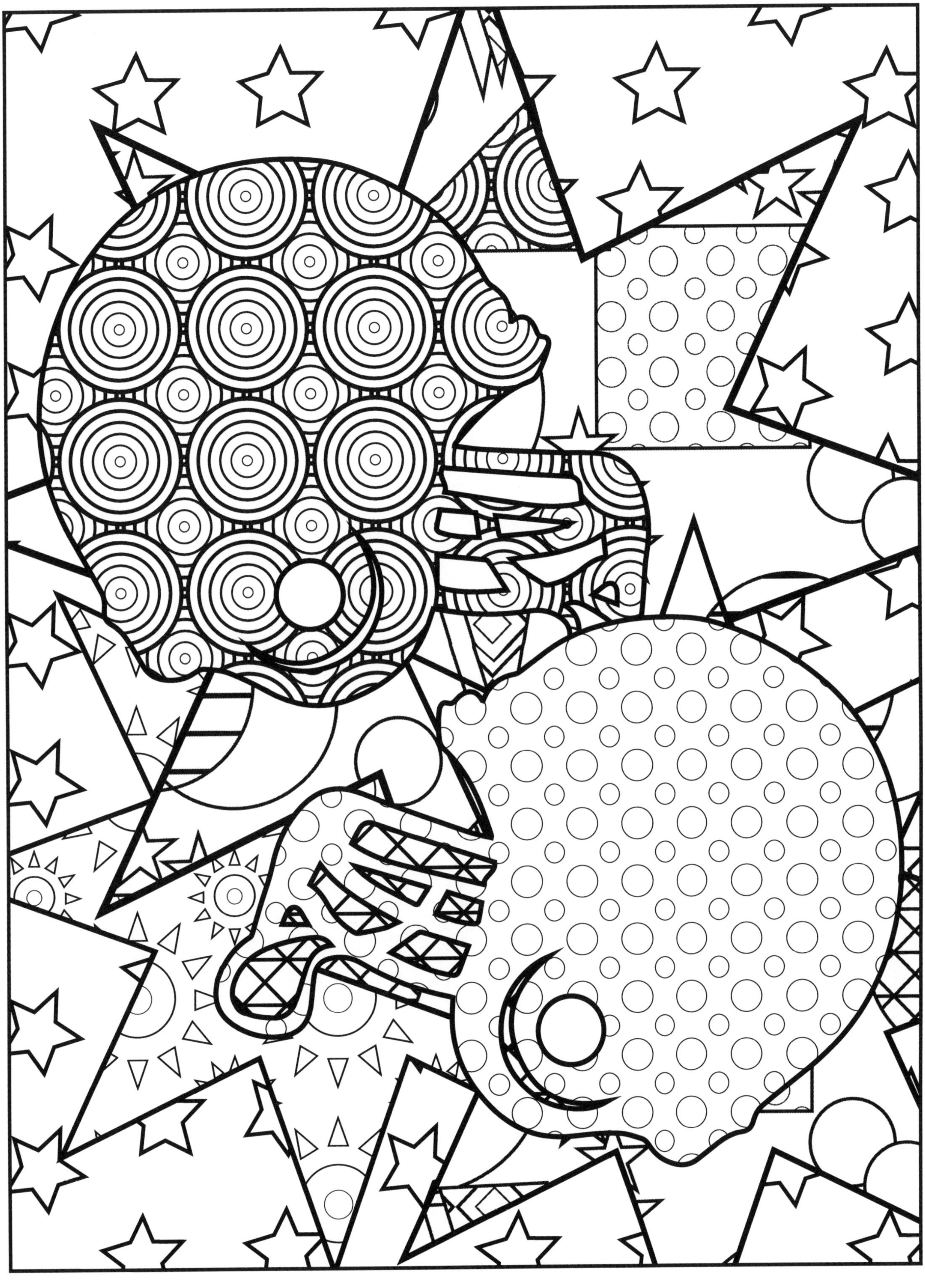

Made in the USA
Monee, IL
01 July 2021

72662771R00037